How to Start Worrying about Your Hereafter and Achieve True Success

Ibn Al-Jawzi

Published by Muddassir Khan, 2024.

Table of Contents

How to Start

Worrying

About Your Hereafter

And

Achieve True Success

Ibn Al-Jawzi

While every precaution has been taken in the preparation of this book, the publisher assumes no responsibility for errors or omissions, or for damages resulting from the use of the information contained

herein.

Preface

All praise belongs to Allah who warned (the people) before punishing (them) and who taught the exegetes the modalities of discipline as well as good behavior.

May peace and blessings of Allah be upon the most esteemed leader and the most honorable teacher, Muhammad (peace and blessings of Allah be upon him) who was sent to the near and far, and upon his Companions and those who followed.

I have noticed that the preachers who are fans of stories have neglected the proper and appropriate stories, those which strike fear into the hearts of people [in order to keep them away from bad deeds] and which motivate them [to accomplish good actions].

Instead, they have opted for fabricated stories.

As a result, most of their narratives are invented (made-up).

And when what they report is authentic, they add false elements (to the authentic report).

The only thing that matters to them is to maintain the elegance of their assembly by all possible means [while neglecting the true purpose of these assemblies].

So, here is what happens following this: the audience leaves without having been warned against the dangers of sins or having a single heart touched or softened.

[In the best case], the protest preacher mentions to his audience that the Mercy of Allah encompasses everything without also reminding them that the Punishment of Allah is severe.

Preachers are known to be specialists in treating the disease of sin.

Their expertise in repairing the moods of hearts is famous.

This is why they instill hope in the heart of the despairing and the fear of Allah in the heart of the heedless – that is those who do as they please.

This is how they treat illnesses, using their opposites as remedies.

I eventually realized that excessive hope, lack of fear of Allah and deluding oneself are illnesses that have contaminated people's hearts.

The treatment of these diseases therefore requires medicine of intimidation and dissuasion.

Indeed, when the heart remains in this dreamy state, treating it with doses of serenity would be equivalent to using, on a person suffering from hypothermia, a medication that lowers body temperature.

It is for this reason that I have collected, in this work, terrifying stories, warnings against sins, stories describing punishments and stories that put the heart in an uncomfortable state.

All this with the aim of making the confident anxious, softening hard hearts, bringing tears to dry eyes, and motivating the lazy.

And it is with Allah that absolute success rests.

Chapter 1: Most of the sinners rely on the Mercy of Allah

It is necessary to know that the majority of sinners and transgressors rely on the mercy, forgiveness and generosity of Allah, while neglecting and ignoring His terrible punishment.

They came to this biased understanding because they wrongly believed that Allah's Mercy was similar to tenderness.

This conclusion appeared to them because they equated the mercy of Allah with the mercy of creation.

They thought His mercy was similar to what a person feels when they see their enemy being tortured.

He feels empathy for him and his heart is therefore softened.

But in fact, Allah's mercy is absolutely not of this kind.

He who seeks forgiveness while insisting on committing sins is certainly like the stubborn person ignoring all warnings.

Ma'ruf Al-Karkhi said: "Hoping to benefit from the Mercy of the one you persist in disobeying is a form of treachery and insanity."

Some of the wise people said:

"Allah has commanded, in this world, to cut off the most honorable part of your body [the hand] for the theft of the equivalent of 5 carats.

No one should therefore feel safe from His Punishment in the afterlife."

In the same vein, know that the intercession of Ibrahim (peace be upon him), the close friend of Allah, towards his father will be refused as well as the request of the Messenger of Allah (peace and blessings of Allah be upon him) to Allah that He forgive his mother. This fact should encourage the ordinary person to remain in a constant state of worry and fear.

This is what Al-Hassan referred to when he was asked: "Why do you cry for such long periods of time?"

He replied: "I fear that Allah will throw me into Hell without He caring."

Another point that should be highlighted concerns the fact that a person can be punished for sins that he may belittle.

It is therefore necessary to start with intimidation.

This is to keep him away from sins before they are committed.

This way, the person will be able to avoid punishment.

Al-Mughirah ibn Makhadish asked Al-Hassan:

"O Abu Sa'id, what should we do about certain people we associate with and who make our hearts in a state of fear [of Allah and His punishment]?"

He replied:

"O you, old man, by Allah, it is better for you that you be in the company of those who incite you to fear until you reach security [in the afterlife] rather than in the company of those who guarantee you security until lest that which you fear [punishment] fall upon you."

Chapter 2: The punishment of those who command goodness without carrying it out themselves

On the authority of Usama ibn Zayd (may Allah be pleased with him), the Messenger of Allah (peace and blessings of Allah be upon him) said: "On the Day of Resurrection, a man will be brought and thrown into the Fire.

His intestines will come out through his belly and he will go around and round in Hell as a donkey turns around a millstone (in the grinding mill).

The inhabitants of Hell will gather together and say: "So-and-so! What is wrong with you? Did you not order us to do what is right and did you not forbid us from doing what is wrong?"

The man will answer: "Indeed, I ordered the right thing, but I myself did not carry it out, and I used to forbid evil while I myself committed it."

Abu Radi' reports: The Messenger of Allah (peace and blessings of Allah be upon him) passed by the cemetery of Baqi' and said: "'Uff to you, 'Uff to you" [an exclamation which expresses disdain] .

I thought he was referring to me with this exclamation, but he negated my assumption and said: "It is not against you, but it is about the grave of a man whom I had sent to collect [alms] from a family, but he kept the fruit [from the alms] to himself and now he has been given a fruit so similar to that (the fruit) which he unjustly took, but it (the fruit given to him in his grave) is made of fire instead."

Chapter 3: The three things that follow the dead

Anas Ibn Malik (may Allah be pleased with him) reports that the Prophet (peace and blessings of Allah be upon him) said: "Three things follow the dead: the members of his family, his possessions (property), and his works (his righteous actions).

Two of them leave and one stays with him.

The people (his family) and and his wealth leave.

His works remain with him."

Anas ibn Malik (may Allah be pleased with him) reports: The Prophet (peace and blessings of Allah be upon him) frequently said: "O You who turns hearts, strengthen my heart (make it firm) in your religion."

He [Anas] continued saying: We asked: "O Messenger of Allah! We have believed in what you have come with. Are you still afraid for us?"

The Prophet (peace and blessings of Allah be upon him) replied: "Yes, certainly the hearts (of the people) are between two of the fingers of the Most-Merciful and He turns them as He wills."

Chapter 4: Warning to Preachers

Anas Ibn Malik (may Allah be pleased with him) reports that the Prophet (peace and blessings of Allah be upon him) said: The night during which I traveled [from Mecca to Jerusalem], I passed by a group of people whose lips were being torn by shears made of Fire.

I then asked: "Who are they?"

They [the angels] replied: "They were preachers in the world, ordering people to do good works, while abandoning good deeds themselves, while they recited the Book (the Quran). Do they then not understand?"

Chapter 5: The punishment of the backbiters

Anas Ibn Malik (may Allah be pleased with him) reports that the Prophet (peace and blessings of Allah be upon him) said: When my Lord raised me to the heavens, I passed by a group of people whose nails were made of copper and who were scratching their faces and chest with them."

I asked: "Who are they O Gabriel? ".

He answered me: "They are those who ate the flesh of people [the backbiters] and defamed the honor of others."

Reported by Abu Dawud and Ahmad.

Authenticated by Al-Albani.

Chapter 6: He never laughs

Anas Ibn Malik (may Allah be pleased with him) reports that the Prophet (peace and blessings of Allah be upon him) asked the angel Gabriel: "Why I never see the angel Mika'il laugh?

He replied: "He has never laughed since Hell-Fire was created."

Reported by Ahmad.

Authenticated by Al-Albani.

Chapter 7: The condition, in the afterlife, of the most prosperous people of this world

———

Anas Ibn Malik (may Allah be pleased with him) reports that the Prophet (peace and blessings of Allah be upon him) said: On the Day of Resurrection, will be brought among the people of Hell the one who was the most affluent in this world.

He will be immersed only once in the Fire.

Then he will be asked: "O son of Adam, have you ever enjoyed a single blessing? Have you ever tasted a single pleasure?"

He will answer: "No, by Allah, O Lord."

Then will be brought the one among the people of Paradise who was the most destitute in this world.

He will immersed only once in Paradise.

He will then be asked: "O son of Adam, have you ever experienced misery? Have you ever endured adversity?"

He will reply: "No, by Allah, O Lord.

I have never known misery or endured adversity."

Reported by Muslim

Chapter 8: The secrets of Al-Barzakh

Al-Baraa ibn 'Azib reports: We went out with the Messenger of Allah (peace and blessings of Allah be upon him) to accompany the mortal remains of a man from the Ansars to his final resting place.

We reached the grave before it was completely dug and we sat with the Messenger of Allah (peace and blessings of Allah be upon him) around the grave, in such silence that it seemed as if birds were perching on our heads.

The Prophet (peace and blessings of Allah be upon him) held a piece of wood (a stick) and he was poking the ground with it.

Then he raised his head and said (two or three times): "Beseech (ask) protection from Allah against the punishment inflicted in the grave."

Then he continued: "When a virtuous servant leaves this world for the Hereafter, white angels come to him from heaven whose faces are as radiant as the sun.

They settle down next to him, equipped with a shroud and a heavenly perfume.

It is then that the angel of death comes and sits near his head and says to him: "O good soul! Come out to enjoy divine forgiveness and mercy."

It then comes out (easily) flowing like a drop of water escaping from the mouth of a waterskin.

When the angel of death receives the soul, the other angels immediately take it and place it in the shroud.

They bathe it in perfume with the best smell of musk on earth.

The angels go back up carrying this soul, and each time they pass by a group of angels, they (the the group of angels they meet) say: "Who is this good soul?" They answer: "It's that of so-and-so's son" using the best names that the deceased had in his life here on earth.

Arriving at the lowest sky, they request the opening (permission to enter) which will be obtained as soon as requested.

At the level of each heaven, the soul is welcomed by the best and accompanied to the next heaven; and this until its arrival in the seventh heaven.

Then Allah shall say: "Record the book concerning my servant in the highest spheres of the seventh heaven.

Then bring him back to the earth since it is from it that I created my servants and it is to it that I will return them and it is from it that I will resurrect them."

Then his soul is brought back to his body, and two angels come to him, stand him up and say to him: "Who is your Lord?"

He shall reply: "Allah is my Lord."

They they ask him, "What is your religion?"

He will reply: "Islam is my religion."

They will then ask him: "Who is this man who was sent to you?"

He will reply: "He is the Messenger of Allah (peace and blessings of Allah be upon him)."

Then they shall ask him: "How did you know?"

He shall reply: "I read the book of Allah and adhered to it and believed in it."

A caller will then say from heaven: "My servant has spoken the truth.

Prepare a bed and clothes for him in Heaven.

Open for him a door (within his grave) leading to paradise so that he can receive the foretaste and the freshness."

His grave will then be enlarged to the extent that he can see.

A man will come to him and say: "Be reassured, this day is the one that was promised to you."

"Who are you, you whose face portends good?"

He (the man) will reply: "I am your good deeds!"

Then he shall say: "Master, bring the Hour so that I can join my family and my possessions."

When an unfaithful (disbelieving/wicked) servant leaves this life for the Hereafter, black angels come to him from heaven equipped with hard towels and who settle down within his sight.

Then the angel of death comes and sits near his head and says to him: "O evil soul! Come out to be the object of Allah's wrath and His displeasure."

The soul then disperses from its body.

However, it is extracted in the same way as wet wool is removed with an iron brush.

The angel of death takes it, then the other angels grab hold of it without waiting and wrap it in their hard towels, which emit the most nauseating odor on earth.

They go back up with this soul and, each time they pass near a group of angels, they say: "What is this bad soul?"

"He's so-and-so's son", they respond, using the worst names with which it was called here below, until they arrive at the lowest heaven.

There, they ask for it to be opened but do not obtain it (permission).

At this moment, the Prophet (peace and blessings of Allah be upon him) recited: "For those who treat Our teachings as lies and deviate from them out of pride, the gates of heaven will not be opened to them."

Allah, the Mighty and Majestic, will say: "Put the record concerning my servant in a register placed in the lowest layer of the earth.

Then bring it back to earth since it is from it that I created humans and it is in it that I will return them and it is from it that I will resurrect them."

His soul will then be thrown away.

Then, the Prophet (peace and blessings of Allah be upon him) recited this verse:

"Whoever associates with Allah, it is as if he fell from the sky and the birds caught him, or the wind threw him into a very deep abyss."

He (the Prophet) continued: It was then that the soul of the deceased was brought back to his body and the angels questioned him in these terms: – "Who is your Lord?

"Well, well. I don't know!", he will reply.

"What is your religion?"

"Well, well. I don't know!"

A caller will say from heaven: "Prepare him a bed and clothes in Hell. Open a door to Hell for him."

A heat and a burning wind then come to him from there and his grave narrows so that his ribs cross.

Then, a man with an unpleasant face, unpleasant clothes and a foul odor says to him: "Be assured that this day is the bad day that was promised to you."

"Who are you, you whose face portends evil?"

"I am your bad deeds."

Then the person (in the grave) shall say: "Lord, do not make the Hour come."

Reported by Abu Dawud & Ahmad.

Authenticated by Al-Albani

Narrated Anas (may Allah be pleased with him), the Prophet (peace and blessings of Allah be upon him) said: "When a faithful servant is laid in his grave, his companions go away and he still hears the sound of their shoes; two angels come to him, sit him down and say to him: – "What does this man, Muhammad (peace and blessings of Allah be upon him) say?"

"I testify that he is the servant of Allah and His Messenger.

"Look at the seat reserved for you in hell. Allah has replaced it for you with a seat in paradise."

The Prophet (peace and blessings of Allah be upon him) added: "He then saw the two seats."

As for the infidel or the hypocrite, both will answer: – "I don't know."

I only said what people said! "May you know nothing and say nothing!"

Then they will strike him with a hammer between the ears and he will utter a cry that every neighboring creature will hear except men and jinns."

Al-Bara ibn 'Azib reports: "While we were with the Messenger of Allah (peace and blessings of Allah be upon him), he noticed a group of people and then asked: "Why have they gathered?"

We replied: "They are digging a grave [for a burial]."

Hearing this, the Prophet (peace and blessings of Allah be upon him) ran to the grave.

When he reached it, he fell to his knees.

So I stood in front of him to see what he was doing.

He cried so much that his tears mixed with the dust.

He then looked at us and said: "O my brothers, prepare yourselves for this day [the day of death]."

'Abdullah ibn Buraydah reported from his father that the Messenger of Allah (peace and blessings of Allah be upon him) came out of his house one day and called out loud three times: "O people, do you know to what example you and I correspond?"

They replied: "Allah and His Messenger know better."

He said: "The example of you and me is like a group of people fearing the attack of their enemy.

They then decide to send a man to investigate the matter.

It is then that the man notices that the enemy is approaching."

Chapter 9: The anguish and concern of 'Umar Ibn Al-Khattab

Abdullah ibn 'Amir ibn Rabi'ah reports: "I saw 'Umar ibn Al-Khattab (may Allah be pleased with him) pick up a straw from the ground and saying: "I wish I was this straw, I wish I had never been created, I wish my mother never gave birth to me, I wish I was nothing, I wish I was totally forgotten."

Al-'Abbas ibn 'Abdul-Muttalib reports: I was the neighbor of Umar ibn Al-Khattab.

I've never seen anyone better than him.

He spent his nights in prayer, his days in fasting and he attended to the needs of the people.

When he died, I asked Allah to make me see him in my dream.

It was then that one night I saw him in my dream coming from the Madinah market.

I greeted him and he returned the greeting, then I asked him: "How are you?"

He replied, "I am well".

Then I asked him: "What did you find [after death]?"

He replied: "I have just finished being judged and my throne [that is his leadership position as a ruler] almost overthrew me, but I found a Merciful Lord."

Zayd ibn Aslam also narrated from Ibn 'Umar that he saw his father in a dream.

He then asked him: "When did you die?"

'Umar replied: "Twelve years ago and I have only just finished being questioned."

Chapter 10: The anguish and concern of 'Umar ibn 'Abdul 'Aziz

Umar ibn Salih al-Azdi reports: I heard an old man from the people of Sham say: Umar ibn 'Abdul 'Aziz entrusted a sack (a bag) to his servant.

When he died, the servant was asked for 'Umar's bag.

However, he refused to give it and said: "There is no good for you inside it."

The case was presented to Yazid ibn 'Abdul Malik who ordered the bag to be brought.

He called the members of the Bani Umayyah to witness the opening of the bag.

When everyone was gathered, he said: "We found a bag that the best of you (Umar ibn 'Abdul 'Aziz) left behind as a deposit."

When they opened the bag, they found inside the pieces of a piece of patched clothing that he used to wear at night.

Chapter 11: The one who cried and made others cry

Yahya ibn Al-Munkadir reports: I heard some of those who knew Muhammad ibn al-Munkadir say: One night while he was praying, his tears were so intense that his family worried about him.

However, this did not lessen his tears, on the contrary they intensified.

His family then asked Abu Hazim to come [to calm him down].

When he arrived, he found him still crying.

Then he asked him: "O my brother, what made you cry so much that you made your family worried about you?"

He replied: "I came to a verse from the book of Allah, Exalted be He, which I recited."

Abu Hazim asked: "Which verse is this?".

He replied: It is the word of Allah, the Most High:

"And there will appear to them, from Allah, what they did not take into account."

Hearing this verse, Abu Hazim was moved and also wept.

When Muhammad ibn al-Munkadir was on his deathbed, he was seized with panic and said: I fear that it will appear to me, from Allah, that which I have not taken into account.

His brother, 'Umar ibn al-Munkadir also used to say: One of the verses of the book of Allah which made me burst into tears is:

"And there will appear to them, from Allah, what they had not taken into account."

Chapter 12: Seeking assistance against the agony of death

Mus'ab ibn 'Uthman reports: Abdul Rahman ibn Abban used to buy slaves, then order his servants to clothe them.

Then he had them brought before him.

He then said to them: "I free you all for the Face of Allah, because I seek your assistance [through the reward I receive from freeing you from Allah] against the agony of death when I face it."

Chapter 13: The reunion of the dead

'Ubayd ibn 'Umar said: When a person dies and is buried, the inhabitants of the grave welcome him and hasten to take information from him, like the people who rush towards travelers upon their arrival.

They then ask him: "What did so-and-so do [during his life]?" He replies: "Has he not joined you?"

They say: "We belong to Allah and we will return to Him, he was sent to Hell."

Chapter 14: Description of the punishment of Hell

Suwayd Ibn Ghaflah narrated: "When Allah wants to neglect the inhabitants of Hell, He assigns to each one a coffin of fire.

Then, He closes these coffins with locks made of fire.

Every time their nerves feel pain, a metal rod is added.

Then, each coffin is placed inside another coffin of fire sealed with a lock of fire and Allah stirs up a fire between them.

Then He again places each coffin inside another coffin of fire padlocked with a padlock of fire and stirs up a fire between them.

So, each of them thinks that no one suffers a punishment more severe than what he suffers."

Chapter 15: A man from among the allies (Awliya) of Allah

Muhammad ibn Bashir reports: Al-Maharibi said: Sufyan told me: "Amr ibn Qays was the one who educated me.

He taught me the recitation of the Quran and (the science of) inheritance.

So I used to come see him in his shop.

When I didn't find him there, I looked for him at his house where I caught him either praying or reciting the Quran in such a way that it seemed like he was taking care of something he was afraid of missing.

When he was not at home, I always found him in the same mosque in the city of Kufa, sitting in a corner crying in such a way that it looked like he had stolen something and hence he had come to hide.

If I didn't find him at the mosque, I found him in the cemetery, crying and blaming himself.

When he died, the people of Kufa closed their doors and marched with his funeral procession.

'Amr ibn Qais appointed Abu Hayyan to lead the funeral prayer, respecting his last wishes.

All the way to the cemetery, Abu Hayyan raised voices in one voice saying: - "Allahu Akbar!".

It was then that everyone present heard a loud voice saying: "Thus comes the doer of good 'Amr ibn Qays."

All of a sudden, the sky was filled with white birds of unparalleled beauty.

The people were amazed and expressed their surprise at the sight of such a number of beautiful birds.

Abu Hayyan said: "Do not be surprised, for it is angels who have come to welcome 'Amr."

Chapter 16: Description of the life of the pious predecessors (Salaf)

'Abd al-Rahman ibn Mahdi reports: Sufyan died at my location. When he was on his deathbed and the agony intensified, he began to cry.

A man said to him: "O Abu 'Abdullah, is it because, seemingly, you have committed too many sins?"

Sufyan picked up something from the ground and said: "By Allah, my sins are less important in my eyes than what I just picked up from the ground.

But I fear that Allah will take away my faith (Imaan) just before I die."

Ibn Abjar reports: When Sufyan was dying, he said to me: "O Ibn Abjar, I am as you see, so take care of those who visit me."

I then brought a group of people back. Among them was Hammad ibn Salamah.

He was standing right next to his head.

Sufyan exhaled and Hammad then said: "Good news to you, for you have conquered what you feared and soon you will meet a Forgiving Lord."

Sufyan said: "O Abu Salamah, do you think that Allah will forgive a person like me?"

He replied: "Certainly, by Him apart from whom there is no deity that deserves to be worshiped except Him."

Listening to these words, Sufyan appeared to be calm.

Ibrahim ibn 'Isa al-Yashkari said: "I have never met anyone sadder than Al-Hassan.

Every time I saw him, I thought he had just been hit by some calamity."

Yazid ibn Hawshab said: "I have never seen anyone more distressed than Al-Hassan and 'Umar ibn 'Abd al-'Aziz.

[Their state of extreme fear of Allah gave the impression] that Hell was created exclusively for them."

Qassim al-Khawwas relates that Muhammad ibn Wasi' said to a man: "What makes you cry is the pre-knowledge of Allah, Exalted be He, about you."

'Amarah ibn Zhadahn reports: Kahmas ibn Al-Hassan said to me: "I have performed a sin for which I cried with regret for forty years."

I asked: "What was that?"

He replied: "A friend of mine visited me one day.

I then bought a fish for him.

After he ate, I got up and took a piece of mud from my neighbor's wall so he could wipe his hands with it.

This sin [taking a piece of mud from your neighbor's wall without asking permission] is why I cried for forty years."

Chapter 17: He will remain in the dust until the Day of Judgment

'Abd al-Wahid ibn Zayd reports: Khabib, Abu Muhammad, was seized with panic when he was dying.

He then said in Persian: "I want to begin a journey that I have never undertaken before.

I want to take a path I have never taken before.

I want to visit my Master and my Lord whom I have never seen.

I want to witness horrors the likes of which I have never seen.

I want to remain under the dust until the Day of Judgment and then stand before Allah.

I fear that He will say to me: "O Khabib, show me a tasbih (the act of saying "Subhanallah") that you have pronounced during the last sixty years without the devil (Satan) dominating you, even if only in part of this word.

What would I answer at that moment?"

'Abd al-Wahid added: "He is a servant of Allah who has worshiped Him for sixty years, devoting his entire life to Allah only and who has never involved himself in the affairs of this world.

What will our situation be like [compared to the him]? Certainly, I seek refuge with Allah! ".

'Abd al-Khaliq al-'Abdi reports: "Utbah al-Ghulam had a house in which he worshiped Allah.

When he wanted to travel to Sham, he condemned his house and said to his people: "Do not open it until the news of my death reaches you.

When he died, they opened it and found a dug grave and metal chains (that is he worshipped Allah reminding himself about the horrors of the grave).

Muhammad ibn 'Ubaid reports: We entered the house of a woman who resided in a district of Basra called 'Afirah.

Some said to her: "Invoke Allah for us."

She replied: "If sinners had been ordered to remain silent, your old lady (that is herself) would never have spoken.

However, a doer of good has asked an unjust one to invoke Allah! I ask Allah to make you taste the food of Paradise and I ask Him to make death dwell in your thoughts."

Chapter 18: Eyes that never dry because of tears

'Abd Al-Rahman ibn Yazid reports: "I asked Yazid ibn Marthid: "Why do you cry constantly?"

He replied: "Why do you ask this question?"

I said: "I hope that Allah, Exalted be He, will benefit me from what you tell me."

He said: "O my brother, Allah, Exalted be He, promised me that He would lock me up in Hell if I ever disobeyed him.

By Allah, if He had just threatened to lock me in the toilet, I would never have stopped crying."

I said: "Is this the state you find yourself in when you are alone, isolated from people?" He said to me: "Why are you asking this question?"

"I hope that Allah, Exalted be He, will benefit me from what you tell me.

He said to me: "By Allah, this fear comes to me when I am about to sleep next to my wife.

It stands like a barrier between me and my desire.

When I am served food, it hits me.

It then stops me from eating.

It continues to haunt me to the point that my wife cries and our children too, because they see us crying without knowing the cause.

It sometimes irritates my wife to the point that she says: 'Woe is me, the excessive state of sadness which overwhelms you in this life has prevented me from enjoying even a single moment at your side.'"

Chapter 19: The sorrow of the Day of Judgment brings tears in the worldly life here below

Sufyan ibn 'Uyaynah said: "Whenever Umayyah al-Shami prayed, he would cry to the point that the sound of his sobs resounded and his tears streamed onto the stones of the ground."

The governor of this province sent him a message saying: "You are harming the prayers of others with your excessive crying and your loud sobbing."

Hearing these words, he burst into tears and said: "Feeling the sorrow of the Day of Judgment has brought forth abundant tears in me which sometimes relieve me."

Chapter 20: Send this message to anyone in distress

'Ali ibn Abi al-Hurr reported: Khashish al-Musili and I entered [Sham] through the gate of al-Jabiyah while I was holding in my hand a letter that I I had received from Hamada the devotee.

It read: "Send my greetings to anyone in distress in Sham."

Hearing these words, Khashish burst into tears as people looked at him.

Chapter 21: The Horrors of the Day of Judgment

Abu al-'Aliyah reports (regarding the horrors of the Day of Judgement that): Ubay ibn Ka'b said: While the people are busy in the market, the sunlight disappears and the mountains disintegrate.

The earth is disturbed and the stars are shaken.

Livestock, birds, and wild beasts begin to mix [out of extreme fear and confusion].

The Jinns tell the humans: "We will bring you news of what is happening."

They head towards the sea and when they reach it, they find an intense and lingering fire.

Then, while they were witnessing this scene, the earth was torn from its first layer to the seventh.

Then the heavens are torn apart from the first to the seventh.

It is then that a wind bursts and carries away their souls."

Muhammad ibn al-Furat reports: I heard Muharib ibn Duthar say: On the Day of Judgment, the birds will flap their wings in confusion and vomit out what they had in their gizzard, but they will not be able to achieve what they are looking for because of the horrors they will witness that day."

Ibrahim al-Harbi reports: Mus'ab told me that his father said: There was a man known for his piety among the people of Madinah.

When he was on his deathbed, he was overcome by panic.

Then the people asked him: "Are you afraid of death despite the many good works you have accomplished?"

He said: "Why should I not be afraid?! By Allah, if the governor of Madinah sent me a messenger, I would panic.

So how should I feel now that I receive the messenger of the Lord of the worlds [the angel of death]?"

Chapter 22: Conversation between the dead

Muhammad ibn Ja'far reports: I heard Muhammad ibn Sabih say: 'I was informed that when a person is placed in his grave [and he has committed sins], he is punished or presented with that which he hates in there.

The dead from the neighboring graves say to him: "O you whose brothers and neighbors had died, leaving you behind in the world, have you not learned from our case (when we died and you were still alive)? Have you not reflected on us as we moved on into death? Have you not noticed that our works were brought to an end by our death, so what did you still have time for? So why didn't you take advantage of what we neglected?"

It is then that the earth calls out to him by saying: "O you who were deceived by the lower world! Why did you not learn lessons from those who were deceived by this life then taken away from it and buried underground?"

Al-Hakam ibn Sinan reports that 'Amr ibn Dinar said: There was a man among the inhabitants of Madinah whose sister died.

So he buried her.

However, after burying her, he remembered that he had left his wallet in the grave when he buried his sister.

He returned with a friend of his and they dug in the grave then he retrieved his wallet.

He then said to his friend, "Stand back for a moment, so I can look at my sister."

He then lifted part of the covering extended at the top and found the grave on fire.

He restored the grave to its original state and returned home.

He then asked his mother: "Inform me about the religiosity of my sister during her life."

She said: "As far as I remember, your sister had the habit of performing prayer late and praying without ablution.

At night, when everyone was asleep, she would go to our neighbors' doors and spy on them, then spread their secrets publicly."

Chapter 23: The horrors of the grave

Hudhayfah (may Allah be pleased with him) reports: "We attended a funeral with the Prophet (peace and blessings of Allah be upon him).

When we arrived at the grave, he sat down at its edge and looked repeatedly inside.

He then said: "The believer will be squeezed in the grave, such that his bones will be broken, while the grave of the disbeliever will be filled with fire."

Abu Sa'idal-Khudri reports that the Messenger of Allah (peace and blessings of Allah be upon him) said: When the funeral procession is ready and the men carry the deceased on their necks (shoulders), if it was pious, then it will say, "Take me quickly".

If he was not pious, then it will say, "Woe is me, where are they taking me?"

Its voice is heard by everyone except humans.

If they heard it, they would lose consciousness."

Chapter 24: Description of the punishment of the grave

S amurah Ibn Jundub reports: The Prophet (peace and blessings of Allah be upon him) once told us: Two angels came to me last night.

They woke me up and said: "Let's go."

So I left with them, and we arrived near a man lying next to whom stood a man holding a big rock.

The latter threw the rock on the head of the first smashing it, while the rock rolled to the other side.

The standing man followed the rock, picked it up and did not return to his place until the head of the man (who was lying and had his head smashed) had regained its initial shape.

He (the one who had thrown the rock) would then come back and do the same that he had done before.

I said to them: "Glory to Allah! Who are these two persons?"

They said to me: "Move on!"

So we left and came to a man lying on his back, while another with an iron hook was standing next to him.

He placed the iron hook in the man's (the one who was lying) mouth and tore off that side of his face down to the back of his neck, and he tore his nose down to the back of his neck, and his eye down to the back of his neck.

Then he moved to the other side and acted in the same way as for the first half of the face.

When he was finished with the second half, the first half had returned to its original shape.

Then he would come back and act the same as for the first time.

I said to them: "Glory to Allah! Who are these two?" They said to me: "Move on."

So we went on, then we arrived in front of a sort of oven – it seems to me that he said: "There were confused noises and voices coming from this oven" –.

We looked inside and saw naked men and women.

A flame came from below them, and when it touched them, they screamed.

I said: "Who are they?"

They said to me: "Move on."

So we went on and came to a river—I think he said it was red like blood.

There was a man swimming in this river, and on the bank stood another man who had a multitude of stones near him.

The swimmer came towards him, opened his mouth, and the other made him swallow a stone.

Then the swimmer would leave again, then he would come back towards him.

Every time he came back, the man from the river opened his mouth - the man from the bank made him swallow a stone.

They said to me: "The first man you passed by and whose skull was smashed with a rock was a man who learned the Quran and did not apply (act on) it, and slept during the obligatory prayer.

The man with whom you passed, and whose mouth was torn out to the back of his neck, his nose to his neck, and his eye to his neck, is a man who left his home carrying a lie which spread to reach distant lands.

The naked men and women in this oven-like construction are the fornicators (adulterers and adulteresses).

The swimmer who was made to swallow stones is the one who consumed riba (usury).

———————

SAHL IBN SA'D REPORTED that the Messenger of Allah (peace and blessings of Allah be upon him) said: "A person can do acts which seem to people to be the acts of the people of Paradise, when in fact he is one of the inhabitants of the Fire (Hell) and Similarly, a person can do acts that seem to people like the acts of the people of Fire (Hell), when in fact he is one of the inhabitants of Paradise.

In truth, works (deeds) depend only on their ends (what a person's last deed is going to be)."

Chapter 25: The state of the sun on the Day of Judgment

Abu Umamah reports that the Messenger of Allah (peace and blessings of Allah be upon him) said:

"On the Day of Judgment, the sun will approach [draw near people] until it is a mile or two from them.

The heat will increase to such an extent that the insects will boil like [liquids] boil in a pot.

People will be overcome with sweat based on their bad deeds.

Among them, some will have their sweat reaching up to both of their heels.

Among them, some will have their sweat reaching up to both their knees.

Among them, some will have their sweat reaching up to their groin.

Among them, some will be bridled by their sweat."

Ibn 'Abbas reported that the Messenger of Allah (peace and blessings of Allah be upon him) said:

"How can I rejoice when the angel responsible for blowing the Trumpet placed the Trumpet in his mouth (preparing to blow) and lowered his forehead, attentively waiting to hear the command to blow into it?"

The Companions (Allah be pleased with them) asked: "What should we say?"

He replied: Say: "Allah (Alone) is sufficient for us and He is the best Manager of our affairs and in Him we place all our trust."

Ibn 'Umar reported: The Messenger of Allah (peace and blessings of Allah be upon him) said:

"Alcohol has been cursed for ten reasons: its essence is cursed, as is he who drinks it, he who pours it for others, he who sells it, he who buys it, he who produced, the one for whom it is produced, the one who transports it, the one for whom it is transported and the one who consumes the money from its sale."

Chapter 26: The Punishment of the Pretentious and Self-Centered

Salim relates from his father that the Prophet (peace and blessings of Allah be upon him) said: "While a man walked arrogantly, admiring his own person along with his clothes, Allah ordered the earth to swallow him up.

He continues to thrust into it until the Day of Resurrection."

Ibn 'Umar reported: I heard the Messenger of Allah (peace and blessings of Allah be upon him) say:

"Whoever happens to be a conceited person full of arrogance or walks in a proud manner will meet Allah, exalted be He, while He is angry with him."

Ibn 'Umar reported that the Messenger of Allah (peace and blessings of Allah be upon him) said:

"Those who depict images [of living beings] will be punished on the Day of Judgment and it will be said to them: 'Breathe life into what you have created.'"

Ibn 'Umar reports that the Prophet (peace and blessings of Allah be upon him) said:

"When one of you dies, he is presented with his place in the morning and evening.

If he is one of the people of Paradise then he is in Paradise and if he is one of the people of the Fire then he is in the Fire and it is said to him: 'This is your place until Allah resurrects you on the Day of Judgment.'"

Chapter 27: The state of the believer in this world

———

Ibn 'Umar reports: The Messenger of Allah (peace and blessings of Allah be upon him) took me by the shoulder and said to me:

"Be in this world like a stranger or a traveler and consider yourself among the dead."

'Abdullah ibn 'Amr reports: The Messenger of Allah (peace and blessings of Allah be upon him) came to us while he was carrying two books in his hands, then said: "Do you know what these two books are?" We replied: "No, unless you inform us about them."

He said about the sheet in his right hand: "It is a book which comes from the Lord of the worlds, exalted be He.

Listed inside are the names of the people of Paradise, as well as those of their fathers and their tribes.

It is sealed so the number neither increases nor decreases."

He then said about the book in his left hand: "It is the book inside which are found the names of the people of Hell, as well as the names of their fathers and their tribes.

It is sealed so their number does not increase or decrease."

The Companions said: "For what reason must we work (do righteous actions and avoid wrong actions) from the moment since the destiny of each person is predestined?"

He replied: "Work, but try to get closer to perfection, because he who is predestined to be among the people of Paradise accomplishes the works of the people of Paradise before he dies, despite the actions he performed before that, and he who is predestined to be among the people of Hell will carry out the deeds of the people of Hell, despite the works he has done before."

Chapter 28: The man whose prayer (Salah) is not accepted for 40 days

'Abd Allah ibn 'Amr reported: I heard the Messenger of Allah (peace and blessings of Allah be upon him) say:

"Whoever drinks a sip of alcohol, his prayer will not be accepted for forty days.

If he repents, Allah will accept his repentance."

The narrator said: I do not know if it was the third or fourth time that he said:

"If he commits (this sin) again, then Allah pledges to make him drink the mud of *khabaal* on the Day of Resurrection."

He was asked: "O Messenger of Allah, what is khabaal's mud?"

He replied: "The secretions of the people of Hell."

'Abdullah ibn 'Amr reported that the Messenger of Allah (peace and blessings of Allah be upon him) said: "[The example of] the one who abandoned a single prayer because he was drunk (intoxicated) is such as he who possessed all this world and that which it contains, before We take it completely away from him.

As for the one who abandons prayer four times due to drunkenness, Allah, exalted be He, undertakes to make him drink the mud of khabaal."

It was asked: "O Messenger of Allah, what is khabaal's mud?"

He replied: "The secretions of the people of Hell."

Chapter 29: When you walk during my funeral

Abu Bardah reports that Abu Musa said during his last wishes: "When my funeral begins, walk quickly.

Do not follow my funeral procession carrying any censers (containers containing hot coal used to burn incense for its flavored smoke and perfume), and do not put anything in my grave that could serve as a barrier between the earth and me.

Do not build anything at the top of the grave.

I also declare to you witnesses that I am innocent of anyone shaving their head, crying loudly or tearing their clothes [in response to my death]."

People asked him: "Did you hear the Prophet (peace and blessings of Allah be upon him) say anything about this?"

He replied: "Yes, I heard the Prophet (peace and blessings of Allah be upon him) speak so."

Abu Musa reported: The Messenger of Allah (peace and blessings of Allah be upon him) said:

"The people will be presented [before Allah] three times.

The first two times, their arguments and excuses will be heard, but the third time the records will fly into their hands.

Some will receive them in their right hand, and some will receive them in their left hand."

Zayd ibn Wahb reports from 'Abdullah ibn Mas'ud that he said: The Messenger of Allah (peace and blessings of Allah be upon him), truthful, worthy of being believed, said to us:

"Surely, the creation of each of you is produced in the womb of the mother for forty days in the form of a drop, then it becomes a blood clot for a similar period, then it becomes a piece of flesh for a similar period.

Then comes to him an angel who breathes his soul and who has been ordered to do four things: to write his sustenance, the duration of his life, his works (actions) and his fate, miserable or happy (whether he will enter paradise or not).

By Him besides whom there is no deity worthy of worship, one of you performs the deeds of the people of Paradise until there is only arms length between him and it [Paradise] then the writing precedes him, he then acts with the actions of the people of the Fire and he enters the Fire.

One (another) of you performs the deeds of the people of the Fire until there is only an arms length between him and it [the Fire], then the writing precedes him, he then performs the deeds of the people of Paradise and he enters Paradise."

Chapter 30: The true modesty and shyness before Allah

Abdullah ibn Mas'ud reports that the Prophet (peace and blessings of Allah be upon him) said:

"You must experience true modesty (shyness) towards Allah".

The Companions replied: "O Messenger of Allah, we feel modesty (that is we are shy of Allah).

The Prophet said: "It is much more than that.

The true modesty (the one who is truly shy) towards Allah (this shyness causes a person to) preserve his head and what it perceives, his stomach and what he desires.

They remember death and its afflictions.

Let him who wants the beyond leave behind the beauty of life here below.

He who does all this is truly modest towards Allah."

Chapter 31: Beware of sins that are minimized

Abdullah Ibn Mas'ud reports: The Prophet (peace and blessings of Allah be upon him) said:

"Beware of minor sins.

The example of minor sins is that of a group of travelers who stopped during their wanderings to rest in a valley.

Then one of them brought a straw.

Another also came to add more and then another until they had gathered enough to cook their meal.

Remember! If a man has to give account (on the Day of Judgment) for his minor sins, they will certainly destroy him."

In another version: "Beware of minor sins, because they accumulate until they destroy the man."

'Abdullah ibn Mas'ud reports: The Prophet (peace and blessings of Allah be upon him) said:

"The people who will be most severely punished before Allah on the Day of Resurrection are the creators of images."

Chapter 32: Will the Fire consume the marks of prostration?

—

Abu Hurayra reported: The Messenger of Allah (peace and blessings of Allah be upon him) said:

"There will be a bridge stretched over Hell.

I would be the first to cross it.

The only invocation that the Messengers will then say will be: 'O Allah, protect us.'

It will be slippery and strewn with pincers and thorns which will scratch people according to their works.

Some will be completely safe, others will only be safe after receiving a few scrapes and some will fall into Hell.

After Allah, exalted be He, has finished judging His servants, He will remove from Hell some of them who testified that there was no deity worthy of worship besides Allah.

He will then order His angels to bring them out.

When the angels look at them, they will recognize them by the marks of prostration.

Indeed, Allah, the Most High, has forbidden the fire to burn the marks of prostration.

They will take them out, their bodies blackened by fire.

They will pour on them water called the water of life.

They will then be reborn like the seed that grows in the silt."

Chapter 33: The first three people admitted to Hell

Abu Hurayrah (Allah be pleased with him) reports that the Prophet (peace and blessings of Allah be upon him) said:

Certainly, the first of the men who will be judged on the Day of Judgment will be:- A man who died as a martyr.

He will be brought and Allah will make him recognize His blessings on him and he will recognize them.

He will say: "And what have you done with these benefits?"

He will answer: "I fought for you until I died a martyr."

Allah will say: "You lie, you rather fought so that it was said that you were courageous and it was said."

Then Allah will order that he be dragged on his face until he is thrown into the Fire.

(The second will be) A man who learned knowledge, taught it and read the Quran.

He will be brought and Allah will show His blessings upon him and he will recognize them.

He will say: "And what did you do with these benefits?"

He will answer: "I learned science, I taught it and I recited the Quran, all for you."

Allah will say: "You have lied, you rather learned the knowledge so that people say that you are a scholar and read the Quran so that people say that you are a reciter, and all this has been said."

Then Allah will order that he be dragged on his face until he is thrown into the Fire.

- (The third person will be) A man to whom Allah has bestowed his generosity and to whom he has given all types of goods.

He will be brought and Allah will make known to him His blessings upon him and he will recognize them.

He will say: "And what have you done with these benefits?"

He will answer: "There is not a single thing in which You like money to be spent on without me having spent it for You."

Allah will answer: "You lie, you rather spent so that people would say that you are generous and that has been said."

Then Allah will order that he be dragged on his face until he is thrown into the Fire."

Abu Hurayra reports that the Prophet (peace and blessings of Allah be upon him) said: "Let him who has wronged his brother in his honor or in any other matter ask him for forgiveness today, before there is no more dinar or dirham.

Otherwise He will take his good deeds and give them to his brother according to the wrong he has done to him, and if he does not have any good deeds, then his brother's bad deeds will be taken and put in his account (will be added to his burden)."

Chapter 34: Constantly remember the destroyer of desires.

A bu Hurayarah (Allah be pleased with him) reports that the Prophet (peace and blessings of Allah be upon him) said:

"Remember the destroyer of desires (death)."

Abu Hurayrah reports that the Prophet (peace and blessings of Allah be upon him) said:

"Whoever takes the size of even a span of hand from a land wrongfully, Allah will order him to dig it down to the seventh earth.

Then He will fence it on the Day of Judgment until He judges between people."

Ibn 'Umar reports that the Prophet (peace and blessings of Allah be upon him) said: "Whoever takes land unjustly will be swallowed up to the seventh earth on the Day of Judgment."

Abu Hurayrah reported: I heard the Messenger of Allah (peace and blessings of Allah be upon him) say:

"A person can utter a word that he thinks is insignificant, but it causes him to fall into Hell (the depth of) a distance of seventy years [in journey]."

Chapter 35: The fire of this world compared to the fire of Hell

A bu Hurayrah (Allah be pleased with him) reports that the Prophet (peace and blessings of Allah be upon him) said: "This fire of yours which burns the son of Adam (in this world) represents one seventieth of the fire of Hell."

They (the Companions) said: "By Allah, our fire is more than sufficient."

The Prophet (peace and blessings of Allah be upon him) said: "It (the Hell-fire) is sixty-nine times more intense and each of its parts is equivalent to the heat of your fire."

'Adi ibn Hatim reported: The Messenger of Allah (peace and blessings of Allah be upon him) said:

"Allah, exalted be He, will speak to each of you without an interpreter.

When you look to your right, you will find the works that you have done (in your worldly life).

When you look to your left, you will only find the works you have done (in your worldly life).

When you look ahead, you will see Hell, so protect yourself from the Fire even by giving half a date in charity."

Chapter 36: The advice of the Prophet (peace and blessings of Allah be upon him) to Mu'adh

———

Mu'adh reports: The Prophet (peace and blessings of Allah be upon him) advised me by saying:

"Do not associate anything with Allah in worship even if (your sins were as grievous as) burning or killing (a person unlawfully).

Do not disobey your parents even if they order you to divorce your wife or give up your property.

Do not abandon an obligatory prayer intentionally, for whoever abandons an obligatory prayer intentionally Allah withdraws His protection from him.

Do not consume intoxicating drinks, for they are indeed the cause of all evil deeds, and beware of sins, for sin brings the wrath of Allah."

'Aisha reported: The Messenger of Allah (peace and blessings of Allah be upon him) said:

"A person can perform the works of the people of Paradise while being, in fact, predestined to belong to the people of Hell.

Before his death, he changes and begins to perform the works of the people of Hell and therefore enters Hell.

A person can do the works of the people of Hell while being, in fact, predestined to belong to the people of Heaven.

Before his death, he changes and begins to perform the works of the people of Paradise and therefore he enters Paradise."

Chapter 37: The Resurrection of people on the Day of Judgment

‘Aisha (Allah be pleased with her) reported: The Prophet (peace and blessings of Allah be upon him) said:

"You will be resurrected on the Day of Judgment, naked, uncircumcised and barefoot."

Aisha asked the Prophet (peace and blessings of Allah be upon him): "Will the men and women look at each other?"

He replied:

"O 'Aisha, the situation will be too worrying for them to look at each other."

Ibn 'Umar reports that the Prophet (peace and blessings of Allah be upon him) commented on this verse:

"The Day when humans will stand before the Lord of the worlds",

saying: "The sweat of the people will then reach their ears."

Abu Hurayrah reports: When the verse:

"And warn the people closest to you."

was revealed, the Prophet (peace and blessings of Allah be upon him) said:

"O people of Quraysh — or something similar — ransom yourselves from Allah, because I can do absolutely nothing for you (I cannot avail you at all) against Allah.

O 'Abbas ibn 'Abdul Muttalib, I can do absolutely nothing for you against Allah.

O Fatima bint Muhammad, ask me whatever you like, but I can do absolutely nothing for you against Allah."

Abu Hurayrah reported that the Messenger of Allah (peace and blessings of Allah be upon him) said:

The Fire of Hell complained to its Lord saying: "O Lord! My parts devour each other!"

Then Allah allowed it to take two breaths, one in winter and the other in summer.

The breath of summer occurs when you feel the most intense heat and the breath of winter occurs when you feel the most freezing cold."

Chapter 38: The lightest punishment of Hell

Al-Nu'man ibn Bashir reports that The Prophet (peace and blessings of Allah be upon him) said: "The least punished person in Hell will have two sandals and laces of fire which will boil his brain like a cauldron."

Shaqiq ibn 'Abdullah reports that the Prophet (peace and blessings of Allah be upon him) said:

"Hell will be brought on this Day by seventy thousand ropes, each rope being pulled by seventy thousand angels."

'Aisha (Allah be pleased with her) reports: Two old women from among the Jews came to me and said to me: "The dead are punished in their graves", but I thought they were lying to me and I didn't believe them at first.

When they left, the Prophet (peace and blessings of Allah be upon him) came to me.

I then told him about the incident.

He (peace and blessings of Allah be upon him) said:

"They told the truth.

The dead are truly punished to the point that all the animals hear (the sound from) their punishments."

Chapter 39: The sanctity of the believers in the Sight of Allah

Abu Bakr (Allah be pleased with him) reports that the Messenger of Allah (peace and blessings of Allah be upon him) said:

"If the inhabitants of the heavens and the earth collaborated to kill a believer, Allah would throw them all into Hell on their faces."

Ibn 'Umar reported that the Messenger of Allah (peace and blessings of Allah be upon him) said:

"People will be resurrected on the Day of Judgment, as when their mothers gave birth to them, naked, barefoot and uncircumcised."

'Aisha (Allah be pleased with her) asked: "May my father and mother be sacrificed for you, will men and women be together (in that condition)?!"

He replied: "Yes."

She said: "How shameful it is! ".

He said: "O daughter of Abu Bakr, what is so surprising to you?"

She replied: "I am surprised at what you mentioned about naked, barefoot and uncircumcised men and women, because then they will see each other."

He said: "O daughter of Abu Quhafah, (at that time) the people will be in a state that will them worry too much for them to look (at each other).

They will keep their eyes fixed on the sky.

They will stay there for forty years without eating or drinking.

The sweat of some of them will reach their feet.

For others, it will reach their knees and for still others it will reach their stomach.

Finally, for some, it will reach their head to the point that they will not be able to speak.

Then Allah will show His Mercy to His servants.

He will therefore order an angel to call in a voice that every human and jinn will hear: 'Where is so-and-so?'.

The person will be taken outside the place of resurrection and people will recognize him.

When he stands before Allah, exalted be He, it will be said to him: "Where are those whom he has wronged?"

Then it will be said to him: "Did you harm so and so, in this and that way, on such and such a date?"

He will respond confirming.

Then, some of his good works will be taken away from him to be given to the victims.

The Day when this will happen no dirham or dinar shall be useful or beneficial.

Rather, what will be used (to compensate the wronged) will be the removal of good works (of he who wronged others) and the addition of bad works (to the record of he who wronged others).

This process of compensating victims will continue until everyone has been compensated.

Then, no one will think that they will survive after seeing the harshness of the interrogation."

Mitraf reports from his father: "I saw the Prophet (peace and blessings of Allah be upon him) praying and then I heard a hissing sound like the hum of a boiler coming from his chest because of his sobs."

Anas ibn Malik reported that the Messenger of Allah (peace and blessings of Allah be upon him) said:

When Allah, exalted be He says:

"Seize him and put shackles on him"

seventy thousand angels that Allah created out of His Wrath immediately seize him and chain him from his head to his feet and then drag him across his face, upon which he says: "Alas, how I wish that [my first death] was the final one!" Then he is dragged to the edge of Hell and when he sees it, he cries out: "How destroyed I am! How destroyed I am!"

Then Allah, exalted be He, says:

"On this day, do not cry for destruction once, but ask for many."

Chapter 40: Their gaze is as swift as lightning

————

'Umar ibn Al- Khattab reports that the Messenger of Allah (peace and blessings of Allah be upon him) said:

"What will you do, O 'Umar, when you find yourself in a grave of four cubits by two and you see Munkar and Nakir appear?"

"O Messenger of Allah, who are Munkar and Nakir?"

"These are the two angels who test people in their graves, whose gaze is sharp as lightning and whose voice resounds like thunder.

Each of them holds a hammer so immense that even if all the people of Mina gathered together, they could not lift it, but for them, it is lighter than this stick I have.

They will question you in your grave.

If your answers are hesitant, they will give you a single blow from their hammer which will reduce you to dust."

"O Messenger of Allah, would I then be in the [physical] state I am in now?"

"Yes, but I hope to benefit you against them."

Abu Hurayrah reported that the Messenger of Allah (peace and blessings of Allah be upon him) said:

"Everyone will have regrets after death."

The Companions asked: "O Messenger of Allah, what will each one regret?"

He replied: "He who has done good will regret not having worked more and he who has acted badly will regret not having reduced the number of his bad deeds."

Chapter 41: He tasted the pain of death for 100 years

J abir Ibn 'Abdullah reports: The Prophet (peace and blessings of Allah be upon him) said:

"There was a group of people who traveled across the land.

During their journey, they passed by a cemetery.

One of them then said: 'Let us pray in two units and then call on Allah to bring back to us one of the inhabitants of these graves so that he can inform us about death.'

They all prayed two units then invoked Allah.

It was then that they saw a man with tanned skin come out of a grave while removing the dust from his head.

Between his two eyes he had the mark of prostration.

He said: 'O you, you have sought nothing other than this.

I died a hundred years ago and the heat of death that I still endure has not cooled since.

I therefore implore you to invoke Allah to return me to the state in which I was previously."

Chapter 42: The harshness of the punishment of the grave and its squeeze

Ibn 'Umar reports that the Prophet (peace and blessings of Allah be upon him) descended into the grave of Sa'd and remained there for a while.

After coming out, he was asked: "O Messenger of Allah, what had held you down there?"

He replied: "Sa'd was squeezed in this grave, so I asked Allah to free him from this constriction."

In another version, Ibn 'Abbas reports that the Messenger of Allah said: "By Him who holds my soul in His Hands, I heard its groaning and I witnessed the dislocation of his bones (because of that squeeze)."

Abu Dharr reports: The Prophet (peace and blessings of Allah be upon him) said to me:

"The people will come in three groups on the Day of Judgment: a group of people who will be fed, clothed and on mounts, a group who will walk and run, and a group of people which will be dragged on their faces by the angels."

Chapter 43: Do you know what Khabal's mud is?

Jabir ibn 'Abdullah reports that the Prophet (peace and blessings of Allah be upon him) said: "Everything that is a intoxicant is prohibited and Allah undertakes to make anyone who consumes intoxicating drinks drink khabal's mud."

The Companions asked: "O Messenger of Allah, what is mud of khabal?"

He replied: "The drink of the people of Hell or the secretions of the people of Hell."

Jabir ibn 'Abdullah reports: "When Sa'd ibn Mu'adh died, we went out with the Prophet (peace and blessings of Allah be upon him).

After the Prophet performed the funeral prayer over him and he was placed in his grave, he invoked Allah for him.

He spent a long time in tasbih (saying Subhan Allah).

We followed him in that then he said "Allahu Akbar" and we repeated after him.

He was asked after all this: "O Messenger of Allah, why did you pronounce tasbih and takbir?"

He replied: "The grave was closing in (getting narrower – squeezing) on this righteous servant until Allah delivered (released) him from it."

Abu Dharr reported that the Messenger of Allah (peace and blessings of Allah be upon him) said: "I see what you do not see and I hear what you do not hear.

Paradise is trembling and groaning and cannot do otherwise, because it does not contain any space the size of four fingers without an angel prostrating his forehead before Allah.

If you knew what I know, you would laugh a little and cry a lot.

You would not sleep with your wives and you would go out on the hills crying out for Allah."

Abu Dharr said: "By Allah, I wish I was just a plant to be chewed."

Chapter 44: The Day when a man will flee from his father

Zadhan reports that 'Abdullah ibn Mas'ud said: On the Day of Judgment, all the servants of Allah, male and female, will be gathered together.

A resounding voice will then say: "Here is so-and-so's son.

Anyone who has suffered wrong from him advance to claim his right."

Women will be happy about this, because they will be able to reclaim their rights from their sons and brothers.

Then Allah will forgive His servants as He wishes for their failings towards Him.

He will overlook them, but He will never forgive His servants for their failures towards the rights of people.

When this person is made available to others, Allah the Most High will say to the people: "Come and restore your rights."

Then, this person will say: "O Lord, worldly life has perished so how can I fulfill their rights?"

Allah will say [to His angels]: "Compensate people by taking from his good works and giving them an amount equivalent to their rights."

If this person was virtuous and had only one atom of good works left, then Allah will multiply this amount until it reaches the level that will allow him to enter Paradise.

On the other hand, if he were bad, not only would all his good works perish, but there would also be people left who would claim their rights.

Then Allah will say: "Take bad deeds from these people and add them to his record of bad deeds and then I will cast him into Hell."

Chapter 45: The reward of those who endure hardships with patience

Hamid Al-Tawil reports that Mutraf ibn 'Abdullah Al-Shukhairi said: "I attended the funeral of someone, but when I When I reached the cemetery, I retreated to a place away from the grave (and cemetery).

I prayed two light units there with which I was not satisfied, because I had the feeling that they were imperfect.

After I prayed, I fell asleep and saw in a dream the man buried in the grave far away from me.

He said to me: "You prayed two units of prayers, but you were dissatisfied with their quality."

I said: "That is true."

He said to me: "You work without knowing it while we (the dead) can no longer work.

Being able to pray two units of prayer similar to the one you just performed is preferable to me to possessing this world and what it contains."

I asked him: "Inform me about the one who has the highest rank among the people (the dead) here (in the cemetery)."

He replied: "They are all good people."

I asked: "But who is the one who has the highest rank?"

He pointed to a grave and I then said in my heart (in the dream): "O Allah, bring him to me so that I can speak to him."

It was then that a young man emerged from the grave.

I asked him: "Are you the best people here?"

He replied: "That's what they say."

I continued: "What led you to be the best among them, for by Allah I do not think that you reached this rank by performing many Hajj, 'Umrah, Jihad or good deeds (because of the fact that he died at a very young age)."

He said: "I underwent great trials which I endured with patience and this is what distinguished me from all the others here."

Ahmad ibn Masruq reports that Muhammad ibn Al-Hussayn said: A man asked a very sick skinny person: - "What made you be in this state?"

He replied: "The terror of death."

I said: "Then make sure you do not enter a dwelling (Hell) in which you will wish for death without being able to find it."

'Imran Al-Khayyat reports: We visited Ibrahim Al-Nakha'ia when he was ill.

When we entered, we found him crying.

We asked him: "What makes you cry?"

He replied: "I am still waiting for the angel of death and I do not know if he will tell me that I am in Hell or Heaven."

Chapter 46: If the agony of death were revealed to the inhabitants of the heavens and the earth

Yusuf reports from Yasin that he said: "If the equivalent of a hair of the agony of death was given to the inhabitants of the heavens and the earth, they would all die.

There will be seventy horrors on the Day of Judgment, each of them equivalent to seventy thousand times the horror of death."

Sulayman ibn Habib reports: I heard Abu Umamah say: Allah positions His Throne on the fourth arch (on the sirat) and then He will say: "By My Glory, no injustice will pass through Me today."

Chapter 47: When death is a mercy

———

Muhammad ibn 'Ali Al-Quhastani reports: Dalf ibn Abi Dalf said to me: After the death of my father (the governor), I saw [in my dream] a person who approached me and said to me: "You must come with me to see the governor."

I then followed him and he took me into a deserted house with dark, rough walls and no windows or doors.

He then took me upstairs and into a bedroom.

It had fire marks on its walls and ashes on its floor.

I found my father there naked as he hid his head between his knees.

When he saw me, he asked in surprise: "Are you Dalf?"

I replied: "Yes, may Allah rectify the affairs of the governor."

Then he began to recite the following verses of poetry:

Inform our family and hide nothing from them

About what we suffered, confined in Barzakh

I have been questioned about everything I have done

So, be merciful about what you suppose about me and about what is to come .

He then said to me: "Do you understand?"

I replied: "Yes, I understood."

Then he recited the following verses:

If we were left without accountability after death,

It would have been the relief of every living being.

But when we die, we will be resurrected,

And we will be questioned about everything.

Chapter 48: Sermons of the Pious Predecessors

Abu Bakr Al-Siddiq used to say in his sermons: "Where are beauty and elegance? Where are those who enjoyed their youth and their beautiful appearance? Where are the kings who built these cities and enclosed them with walls? Where are the war winners? They have all perished and ended up in the depths of the dark grave! Hurry and hasten (to do good deeds), but death is quicker."

'Ali ibn Abi Talib often said: "You have been created by the Power of Allah and He is certainly your Lord, whether you accept Him or not.

You will be prisoners in your graves and will end up in ashes.

Each of you will be resurrected apart from the others.

So, may Allah have mercy on him who committed a sin, but immediately recognized that he had done wrong, who feared Allah and then hastened to do good, who was prudent and initiated good deeds, who lived long and therefore contemplated on this, then responded to the call of his Lord and returned to Him, (the one) who examined his evil deeds and repented without delay and prepared himself for the Day of Judgment.

He thus stored the supplies he needs when the time to leave this life arrives.

He decided on the final destination and evaluated his needs and his faults.

He therefore accomplished many good works in order to find them before him when he died.

Therefore, pave the road so that you can walk on it, because only the fruits of old age follow youth, and only sickness follows good health.

Nothing awaits the living except the nearness of the end, the insomnia of the passage from one life to another, the sound of groans, the sweat of brows, the lengthening of noses, the knowledge of anguish, the last denier breaths, the pain of souls reaching the throats and the hearts torn by the love of this lower world.

O you who are still alive, be diligent [in worship] and think of the imminent punishment of the Hereafter.

Fear Allah, for surely He is sufficient as Avenger and He sees everything.

Paradise is enough as a reward and Hell is enough as a punishment.

The Book of Allah is sufficient proof against all."

Ibn Mas'ud said: "You are in the cycle of day and night.

Your life is diminishing, but your works are recorded.

Death will come to you suddenly.

Therefore, whoever has cultivated good will soon enjoy the harvest of happiness and whoever has cultivated evil will soon reap the fruits of regret."

Abu Al-Darda said: "Why do you build houses that you will not inhabit? Why do you accumulate what you will not eat? Why do you hope for what you will not achieve? Those who preceded you built, accumulated and hoped, but their hope was destroyed, what they had accumulated perished and their constructions became graves."

Abu Bakr Al-Tamimi reports: While Sulayman ibn 'Abd Al-Malik was in the Sacred Mosque, someone presented him with a stone on which scriptures were engraved.

So he asked someone to read them to him.

They demanded Wahb Ibn Munabbih who accepted.

Inscribed were the following words: "O son of Adam, if you knew how near your death is, you would have abandoned your distant hopes.

You would have wanted to do more good deeds and you would have been less attached to this world.

If you were not on the right path, you will soon encounter regret when your family and your servants place you in your grave.

Your dearest children will leave you there alone.

Your father and your in-laws will reject you completely, you will be no longer able to return to your life and increase the number of your good works.

So, strive and increase your efforts towards the Day of Judgment before you are drowned in sorrow and regret."

Wahb ibn Munabbih often said in his sermons: "O son of Adam, there is nothing more powerful than the Creator.

There is nothing weaker than the created.

No one dominates the one who controls his business.

No one is more fragile than someone whose affairs are controlled by another.

O son of Adam, yesterday someone close to you died suddenly and today you have a friend whose departure from this life is near.

O sons of Adam, the inhabitants of this world are travelers and must not rest before reaching their destination.

Indeed, eternal abode is found after death."

Al-Hassan often said: "This life passes while our works remain like necklaces worn around our necks.

The best of you are dead, so what are you waiting for? Are you waiting to meet death in person?"

Al-Walid ibn Muslim reports: Some of the caliphs said, while they were standing on the pulpit: "O slaves of Allah, fear Allah as much as you can.

Be like a group of people who were warned of the presence of the enemy and therefore were on guard.

They knew that this life is not a place to stay, so they opted for what is better.

Expect death soon, because it is not far from you.

Get ready to leave, because soon you will be no more.

Certainly, a life that needs extra time and is ruined by its end deserves to be short.

The absent one who is sought for by night and day deserves a quick return and the happiness or affliction that is to come deserves to be prepared for it with fervor.

The servant of Allah must therefore fear his Lord.

He must be of good advice for himself and return to Allah in repentance.

He must control his desires, because the moment of death is unknown.

His hopes deceive him and the devil influences him.

He pushes him to delay his repentance and aggrandizes his bad deeds and sins in order to keep him busy until the sudden arrival of an unexpected death.

Certainly, the line that separates you from Hell and Paradise is death.

Woe then to him whose life was a proof against him because of his negligence and whose days he spent led to his destruction in the afterlife.

I ask Allah to include you and me among those whose sins do not distract from obedience, among those who recognize the favors and grace of Allah and among those who will not know affliction after death.

He is, indeed, the One Who Hears all the supplications of His servants."

Chapter 49: Time passes and every moment counts

A Bedouin advised his son: "Time does not have to warn you and the days do not have to warn you.

Every moment that passes counts, as does what you do with it.

With every breath your life diminishes.

The actions that are most valuable to you are often those that are most painful to you."

People visited a worshipper and said to him: "We would like to question you so answer us."

He said to them: "Ask, but do not exaggerate, because a day that passes never comes again.

Life will never be returned and he who seeks is sincere and worthwhile in what he pursues."

They said: "On what basis will creation be judged on the Day of Judgment?"

He replied: "On their intentions."

They said: "What will we face next?"

He said: "To the deeds you have accomplished (in your worldly life)."

They said: "Advise us."

He replied: "Take with you only what you need for this journey, because the best provisions are those which will help you reach the destination you desire."

Rajab asked a worshipper to advise him.

Then the monk said to him: "Spare no effort that can be profitable for you, do not compromise your good works for people, respect the limits of Allah when you are dominated by your desires, rise to what He loves despite the difficulties that you may face and do not seek the satisfaction of anyone other than Him. Peace."

When Alexander arrived at the place of the barrier, he said to the people present: "Take me to the one who devotes himself most to worship."

They said: "There is a man in this valley who cries so much that plants grow from his tears."

When he went down to meet him, he found him prostrating, saying: "Take my soul and leave my body lying on the ground.

Leave me in oblivion and do not resurrect me on the Day of Judgment."

'Ata Al-Sulami was known for his incessant crying and sobbing.

One day, some of his friends came into his house when the ground was wet at his feet.

One of them thought that he had just performed his ablutions.

However, he (the one who thought this) was informed that it was his tears.

It is reported that he once cried in his room so much that his tears flowed into the gutters of his house and fell on people walking in the street.